THE Moonflower

Published by
PEACHTREE PUBLISHERS, LTD.
494 Armour Circle NE
Atlanta, Georgia 30324

Jacket illustration by Jean Loewer
Book and cover design by Regina Dalton-Fischel

Manufactured in China

10 9 8 7 6 5 4 3 2 1
First Edition

Library of Congress Cataloging-in-Publication Data
Loewer, H. Peter
    The moonflower / Peter Loewer ; illustrated by Jean Loewer. —1st ed.
      p. cm.
    Summary: A brief look at some of nature's nocturnal behavior including the blooming of the moonflower, how moths drink, how bats "see," and how vines climb.
    ISBN 1-56145-138-X
    1. Moonflower—Juvenile literature. 2. Nocturnal animals—Juvenile literature. 3. Night-flowering plants—Juvenile literature. [1. Moonflower. 2. Nocturnal animals. 3. Night-flowering plants. 4. Night.] I. Loewer, Jean, ill. II. Title.
SB413.M65L63 1997
574.5—dc20   96-35976
                              CIP
                              AC

THE Moonflower

Peter and Jean Loewer

PEACHTREE

ATLANTA

When the sun has set in the west...

...but the sky is still too bright for most stars to shine, the buds on the moonflower vine are closed tight. A bumblebee that cannot find the way to his underground home curls up in a flower to wait for dawn.

Bumblebees often live in nests of grass found in small hollows or abandoned mouse homes. In the bright daytime their compound eyes can see landmarks like streams or dead trees that can guide them back to their nests, but at night the light from the moon and stars is too dim for them to find their way home.

3

Crickets do not actually sing, but male crickets can chirp by using their wing-covers like a violin. The cricket plays his song by drawing one wing-cover across the other. If you count a cricket's chirps for 15 seconds and then add 40 to that number, you will know the approximate temperature in degrees Fahrenheit.

It's not really dark yet, but people turn on house lights, children park their bicycles at the back door, and crickets in the yard begin to sing.

4

Bats now wake from their daytime sleep, ready to swoop and glide, catching insects in the gathering darkness. The fireflies of summer will soon begin to send their flashing codes, shining like flying sparklers.

Bats use a kind of radar to see in the dark. They find their way by making high-pitched squeaks that bounce off of insects and other objects. Their large ears pick up the echoes that guide the bats to their prey and away from obstacles.

7

Fireflies, or lightning bugs, use a blinking glow to communicate with each other. The male firefly flashes a special code that only female fireflies of the same species understand. The female firefly waits a few seconds before sending out her own series of flashes. A firefly's glow is produced by a small light organ at the tip of its abdomen.

8

The summer moon rises to the song of a mockingbird and the stars shine in the purple twilight. Fireflies begin to flicker. A nighthawk silently glides across the darkening sky in search of insects to eat.

On this warm summer night the twining moonflowers begin to open, like a movie in slow motion. Wider and wider the petals unfurl under the moon's silvery light.

Vines climb in many ways. Some anchor themselves with thorns and some hold on with grasping tendrils. Others, like moonflowers, wind their stems around fences, posts, or tree branches as they climb and grow. Some vines twine to the left, but moonflowers twine to the right, climbing by twisting their stems around anything that can support them.

11

Moths have a good sense of smell, but they do not have noses. Moths detect odors using their fine, feathery antennae. These antennae, or feelers, react to the scents released into the air by night-blooming plants. Antennae are also important to the moth's sense of balance. If a moth loses its antennae, it becomes lost and cannot fly.

The perfume of the moonflowers floats out on the warm night air. Suddenly the hawkmoths appear, drawn by the sweet fragrance of the blossoms. The hawkmoths flit from flower to flower, their wings blurred with speed.

Many different insects delight in feeding at night-blooming flowers, but the whir of a hawkmoth's wings and the speed of its flight scare other insects away from the moonflowers. While flying among the flowers, the moths pick up pollen and it falls on the blossoms like golden dust.

A moth has a very long, hollow tongue called a proboscis. A hawkmoth tongue is as long as its body, but it is usually tightly coiled to save space and to help the hawkmoth fly faster. The hawkmoth can unwind its tongue like a thin soda straw, plunging it deep into a flower in search of nectar.

15

Owls, like many other animals that are nocturnal, or active at night, have eyes that are far more sensitive to light than human eyes. Owls can see clearly in very dim light because of a layer of special cells at the back of their eyes that acts like a mirror. This mirror doubles the amount of light that owls can use for seeing.

An owl calls and swoops low over an open field. A mouse runs to hide in the shrubbery thicket. The moon climbs higher and higher, and the moonflowers continue to lift their blossoms to its glowing light. The Milky Way spins a mist of stars across the sky.

By four o'clock in the morning a soft glow appears in the east. Suddenly everything is hushed and silent. The hawkmoths have flown away to hide from the light of day. They rest in the bushes and trees, blending in with the bark or sleeping behind leaves.

The moon begins to set and the sun will soon rise. The moonflowers wilt in the early morning sunlight, but new buds are waiting to open the following night.

By the time a moonflower wilts, the process of forming seeds has already begun. Pollen from the stamens of another moonflower plant has been moved to this flower's pistil by the tongues and feet of the hawkmoths. The pollen fertilizes the flower. Although the petals fall away, new seeds will grow in the body of the flower.

19

After the moonflower petals are gone, the part of the flower that remains will grow larger and larger as it forms a seed pod. In a few weeks, the pod will turn dark brown, become dry, and split open, allowing many seeds to tumble out.

The mourning doves coo and the robins sing. An alarm clock buzzes and the kitchen light comes on. The sky grows brighter and brighter.

The hawkmoths, the bats, and the budding moonflowers will sleep through the day, waiting for the night to come again. Then the bats will swoop and the hawkmoths will soar and new moonflowers will open, their trumpets unfurling to the song of the mockingbird and the whir of the hawkmoth's wings.

Nocturnal animals find dark places to rest or sleep during the day. Moths fold their wings and sit silently, hidden underneath a leaf or clinging to a leafy branch. Bats spend the day in natural caves, in attics, or in abandoned buildings. Owls sleep in caves or hollow trees. When the sun sets, these animals will once again come out to hunt and explore.

23

PLANTING A MOONFLOWER

Moonflowers are very easy to grow. Soak the seeds in warm water for a day and a night before planting. This weakens the outer seed coat and helps the seed to germinate and grow. The next day plant three seeds in a three-inch-wide peat pot; plant three to make sure at least one seed germinates. Use a moist mix of clean potting soil.

Put the pots in a warm place (around 65° to 70°F), and make sure the soil stays moist but not wet. You may cover the pots with a piece of plastic wrap and make a little greenhouse. Do not put the pots in the hot sun.

The seeds will germinate and poke up leaves in about five days. Select the largest and strongest of the three plants and remove the other two. Keep the plants inside until the garden soil is warm and there is no danger of frost.

Then go out to the garden and pick a spot that will get full sun at least half the day. Plant the peat pot and its moonflower vine in a hole that will contain the whole pot. You can also grow the plant in a large clay pot (six inches wide or more). Make sure you provide something for the plant to climb upon—strings, stakes, or a fence will do.

As soon as the days are hot and the nights are warm, your vine will begin to grow with great speed. It can easily grow up to ten feet or more in a season. Keep your moonflower plant well watered, and give it some liquid fertilizer every two or three weeks, following the package directions.

Moonflower seeds can be bought from most large garden centers or ordered through the mail from a seed catalog.

Words To Know

Abdomen (p.8): The hindmost section of an insect's body. (In humans, the abdomen is the part of the body between the chest and hips.)

Antennae (p.12): Flexible, feeler-like projections on the head of an insect, such as the *hawkmoth*.

Bat (p.7): A *nocturnal*, winged animal with a mouse-like, fur-covered body. Bats at rest hang upside-down, gripping a branch or a crack in the rock with their feet.

Bumblebee (p.3): A large black bee with yellow markings that makes a pleasant buzzing sound as it flies. Bumblebees carry *pollen* from one flower to another so the flowers can produce seeds.

Compound eye (p.3): A sight organ made up of many single eyes crowded close together. A *bumblebee* has two compound eyes, one on either side of its head.

Cricket (p.4): A common insect that is often found outside on summer nights. Cricket songs are soft and high-pitched.

Fahrenheit (p.4): The common measure of temperature in the United States. Water freezes into ice at 32° Fahrenheit and boils at 212° Fahrenheit.

Germinate (p.24): To develop and grow. With enough light, warmth, and water, seeds will grow and send out shoots and roots.

Hawkmoth (p.12): A hairy, medium-to-large moth with a long *proboscis*. The hawkmoth family includes some of the fastest fliers of all moths.

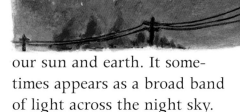

Milky Way (p.16): The galaxy that includes our sun and earth. It sometimes appears as a broad band of light across the night sky.

Mockingbird (p.8): A medium-sized gray and white bird with a slender, down-curved beak. It usually sings from high, open perches, and it imitates phrases from other birds' songs.

Moonflower (p.11): A climbing vine in the morning glory family with heart-shaped leaves. The moonflower's large white blooms that open in the evening are pollinated by night-flying insects like the *hawkmoth*.

Mourning dove (p.20): A gray-brown bird with a small head and a long pointed tail. Its mournful song, "coah, cooo, cooo, coo," is often heard in late evening or early morning.

Nighthawk (p.8): A slim-winged, gray-brown bird that is active at night. Nighthawks feed on insects.

Nocturnal (p.23): Active at night.

Owl (p.16): A *nocturnal* bird with large eyes and with plumage so soft that it can fly almost without a sound.

Pistil (p.19): The female part of a flower that contains the ovules, or future seeds. *Pollen* must reach the pistil for seeds to form.

Pollen (p.15): Fine, powdery, usually yellow grains that are produced by the male part of a flower. Pollen must join with the ovules (this is called pollination) for future seeds to form.

Proboscis (p.15): The long, slender mouthpart of an insect, used like a soda straw to move food to the insect's stomach.

Robin (p.20): A common red-breasted thrush often seen walking about looking for worms on lawns. Its clear and pleasant song includes sounds like "tyeep" and "tut-tut-tut."

Stamen (p.19): The male part of the flower. It is made up of a stalk with a sac at the tip where *pollen* grains grow.

Tendril (p.11): A threadlike part of a climbing plant that is used for support. Tendrils twine around objects and hold on like gripping fingers.

Wing-cover (p.4): The front pair of wings in many insects that have developed into covers. These covers are often beautifully marked and colored, and they fold over to protect the flying wings.

DATE			